BBQ Picnic Days
LINE ART PATTERNS
by Annie Lang

Fire up the grill and grab your favorite picnic supplies because it's time for a backyard barbeque! Choose from dozens of mix and match bbq chickens, piglets and ant characters along with a selection of grills, snacks, and iconic bbq supply themed designs created from Annie's BBQ Picnic Ants, BBQ Chickens and BBQ Pork image collections.

Simply trace the design and then transfer the image onto your project surface to make outstanding personalized items with professional results every time.

Transferring the linework designs

Trace the design of your choice with pencil and tracing paper. Place transfer paper under the tracing paper and place onto your selected surface. Hold in place with tape if necessary. Retrace over the linework to transfer the design onto the project. For fabrics, trace the design, flip the pattern over and retrace the lines using a fabric transfer pen. Follow manufacturer's direction to iron the design onto your chosen fabric item.

Color or paint these designs with

Craft paints, watercolors, markers, coloring pencils, chalks, inks, fabric pens, paint pens, or crayons

These designs are great for

Home Dec Items like furniture, cabinets, accent items, walls, lamps, glassware, kitchen accessories, office and desk items, bathroom accents, cabinets, patio pots and outdoor items, etc.
Fabric and wearable items like t-shirts, sweatshirts, aprons, canvas shoes, totes, quilting squares, table linens and napkins, window and shower curtains, pillows, etc.
Paper Craft Projects like greeting cards, scrap page elements, tags, labels, stationery items, ornaments, gift bags, etc.

For more ideas and designer tips, please visit my Blog at
http://annielang-anniethingspossible.blogspot.com/
My Pinterest Board at http://www.pinterest.com/anniethings/
or my Facebook Page at
http://www.facebook.com/anniethingspossible

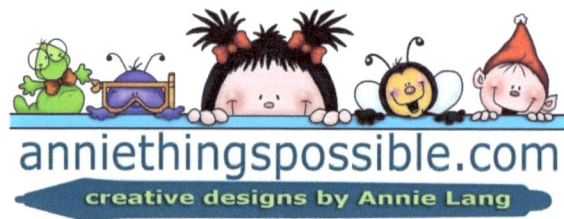

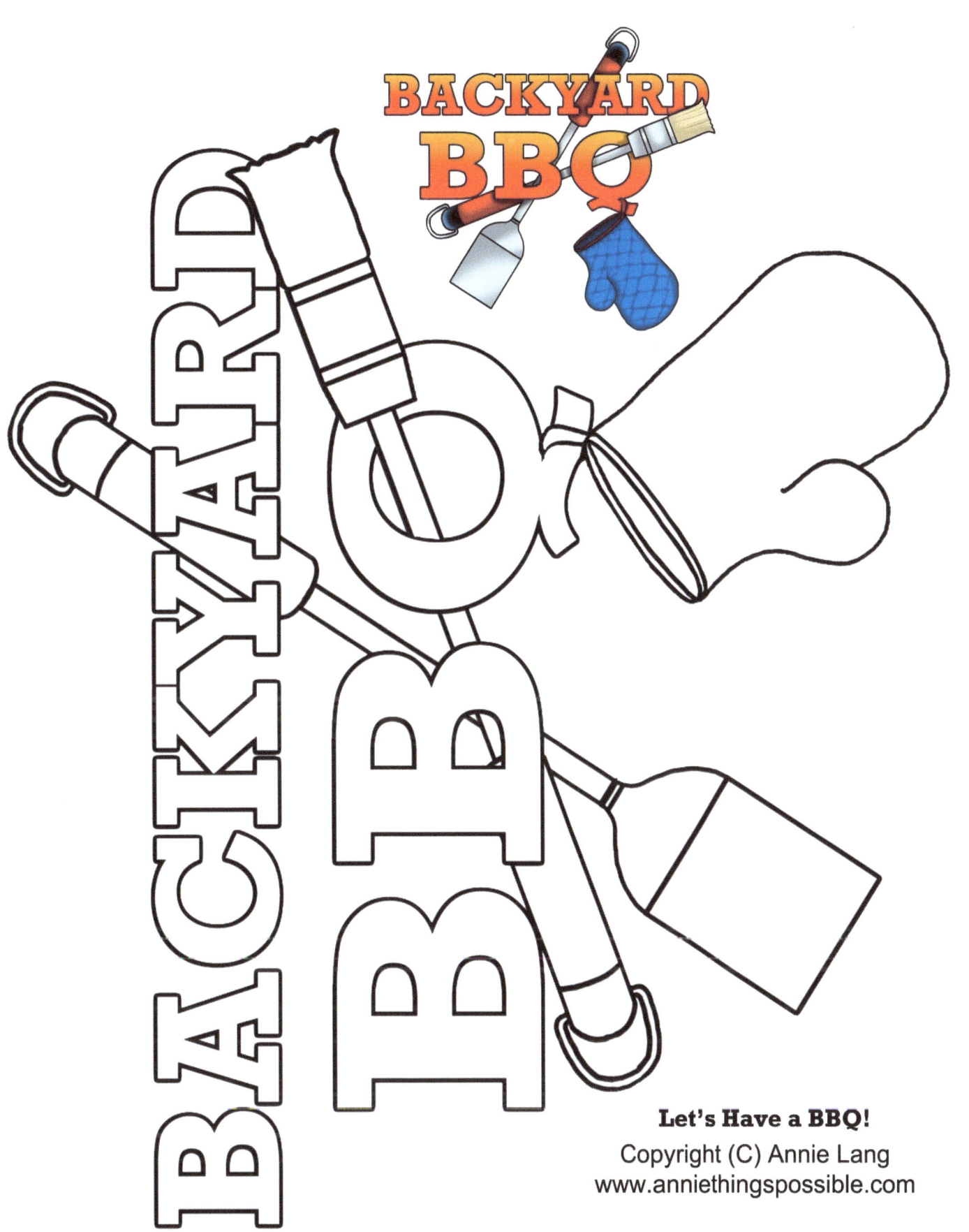

Let's Have a BBQ!
Copyright (C) Annie Lang
www.anniethingspossible.com

Let's have a PICNIC

(C) Annie Lang
www.anniethingspossible.com

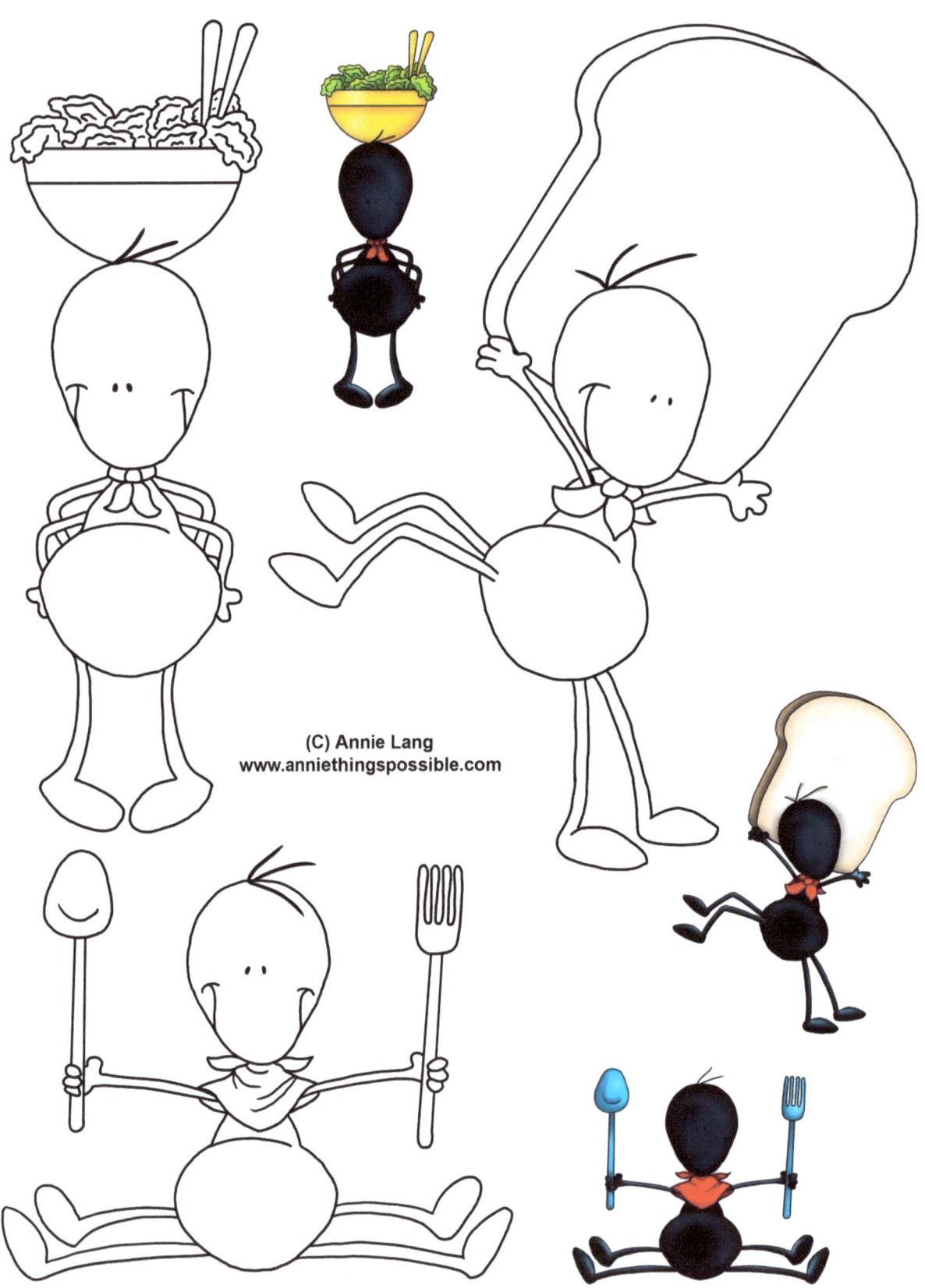

(C) Annie Lang
www.anniethingspossible.com

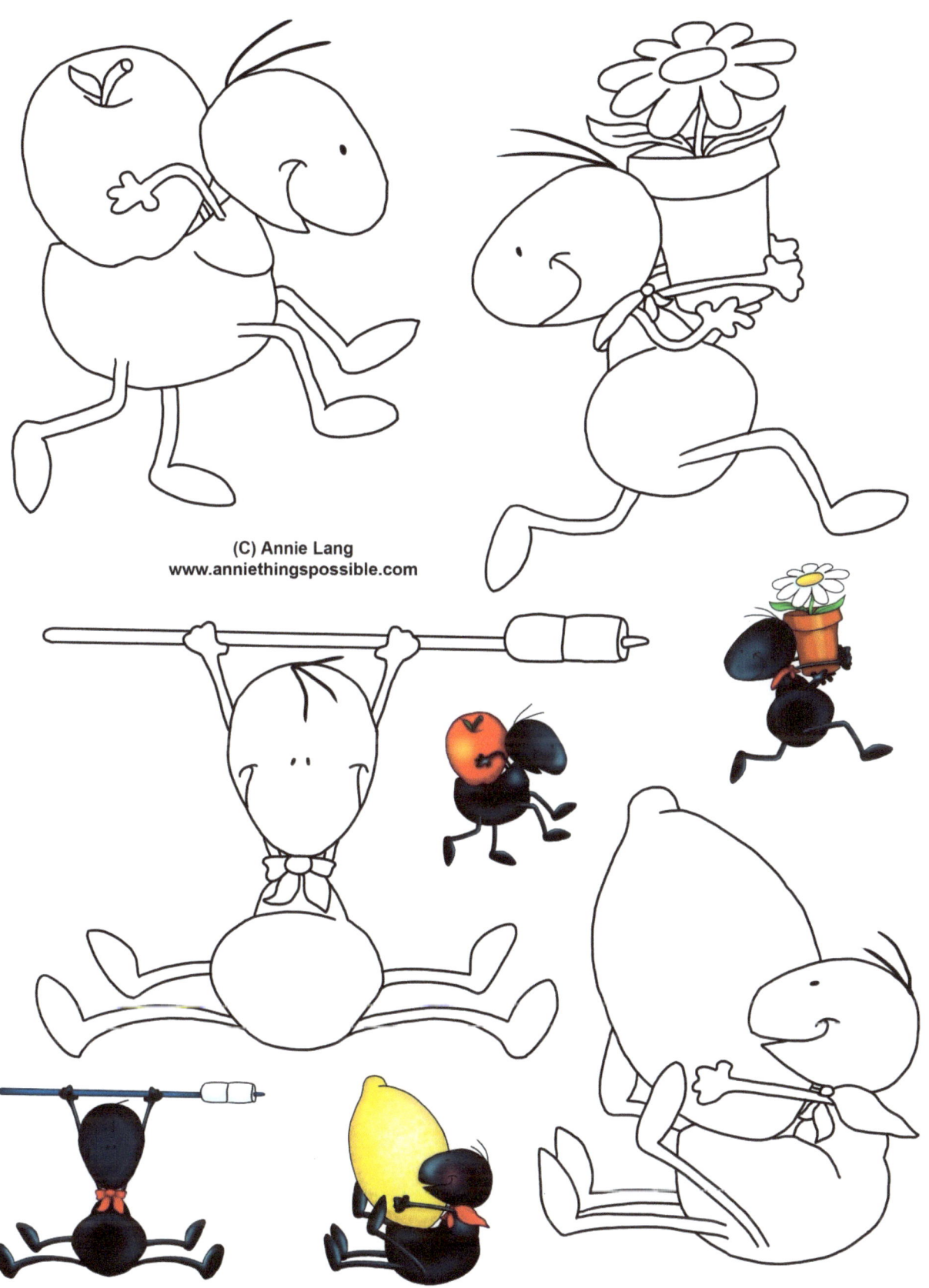

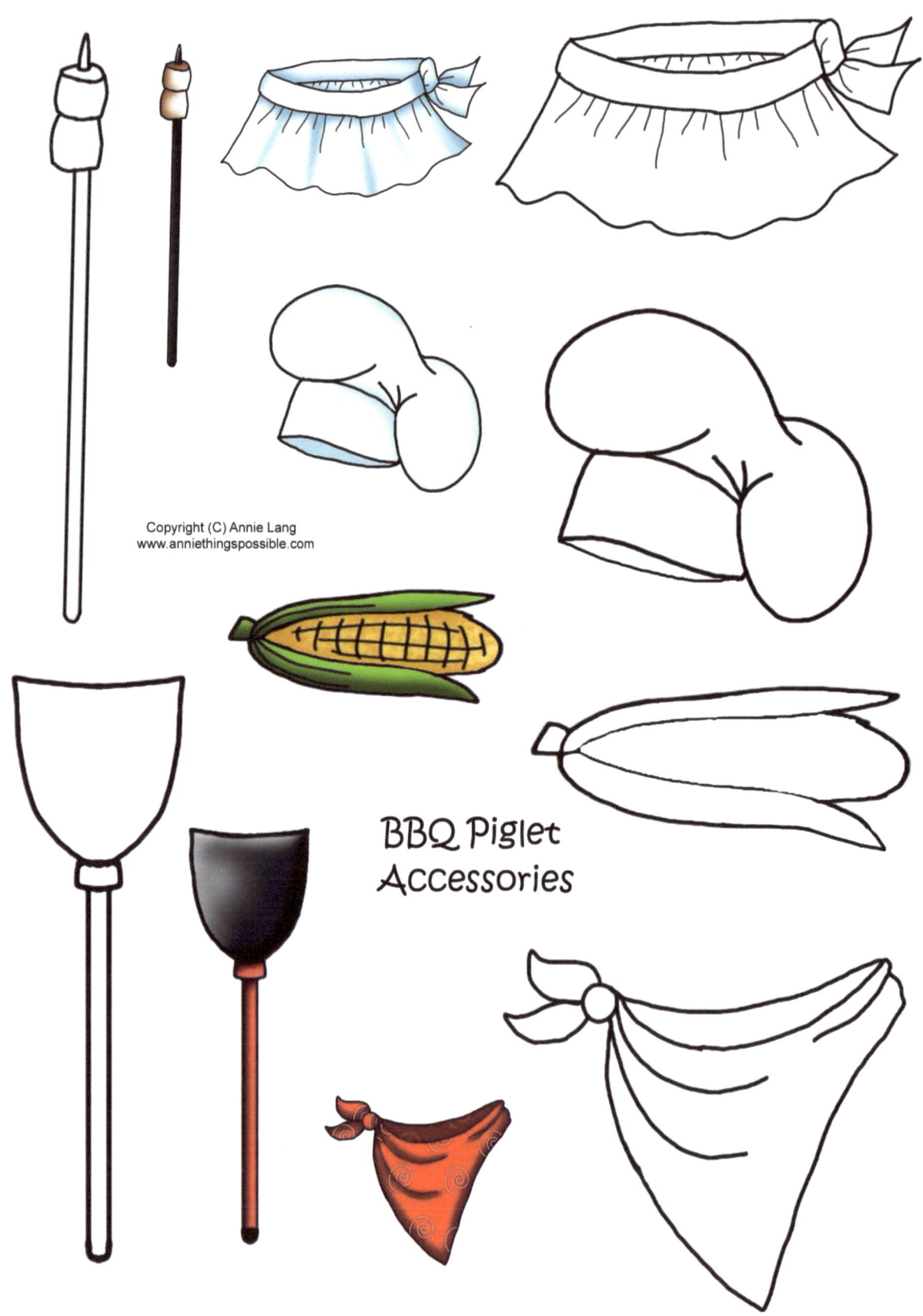

BBQ Piglet
Accessories

Copyright (C) Annie Lang
www.anniethingspossible.com

BBQ
Necessity
Items

Copyright (C) Annie Lang
www.anniethingspossible.com

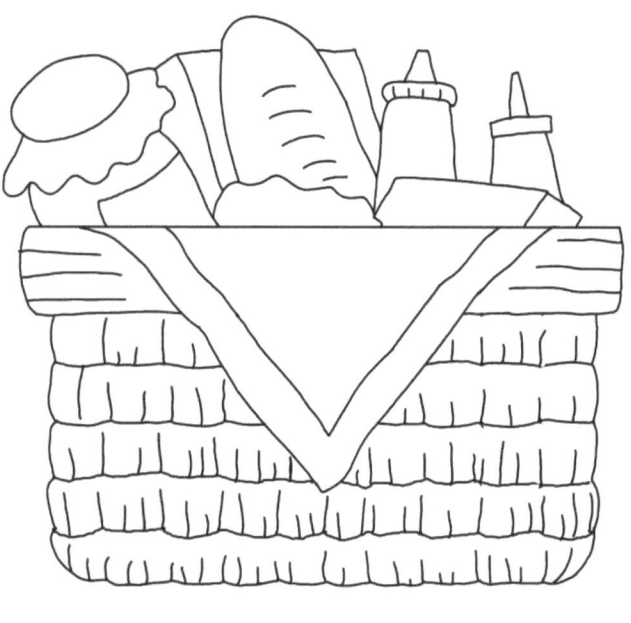

BBQ Piglet Supplies

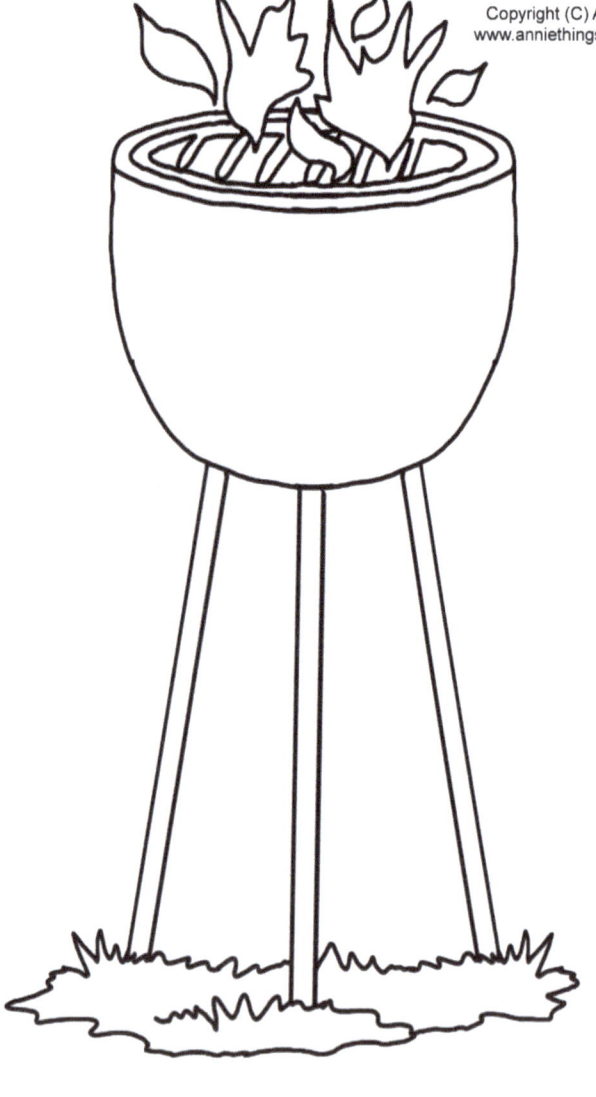

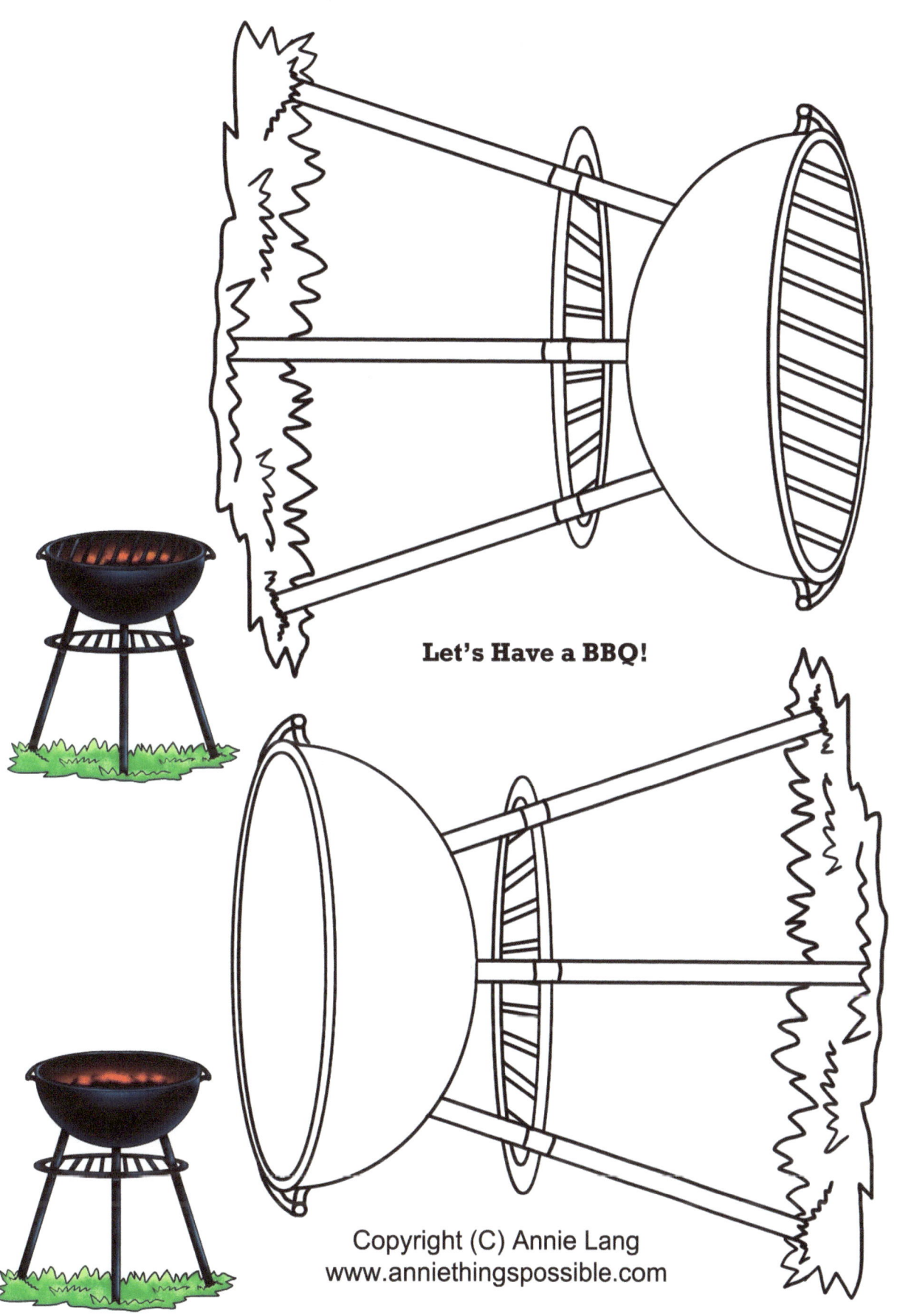

Let's Have a BBQ!

Let's Have a BBQ!

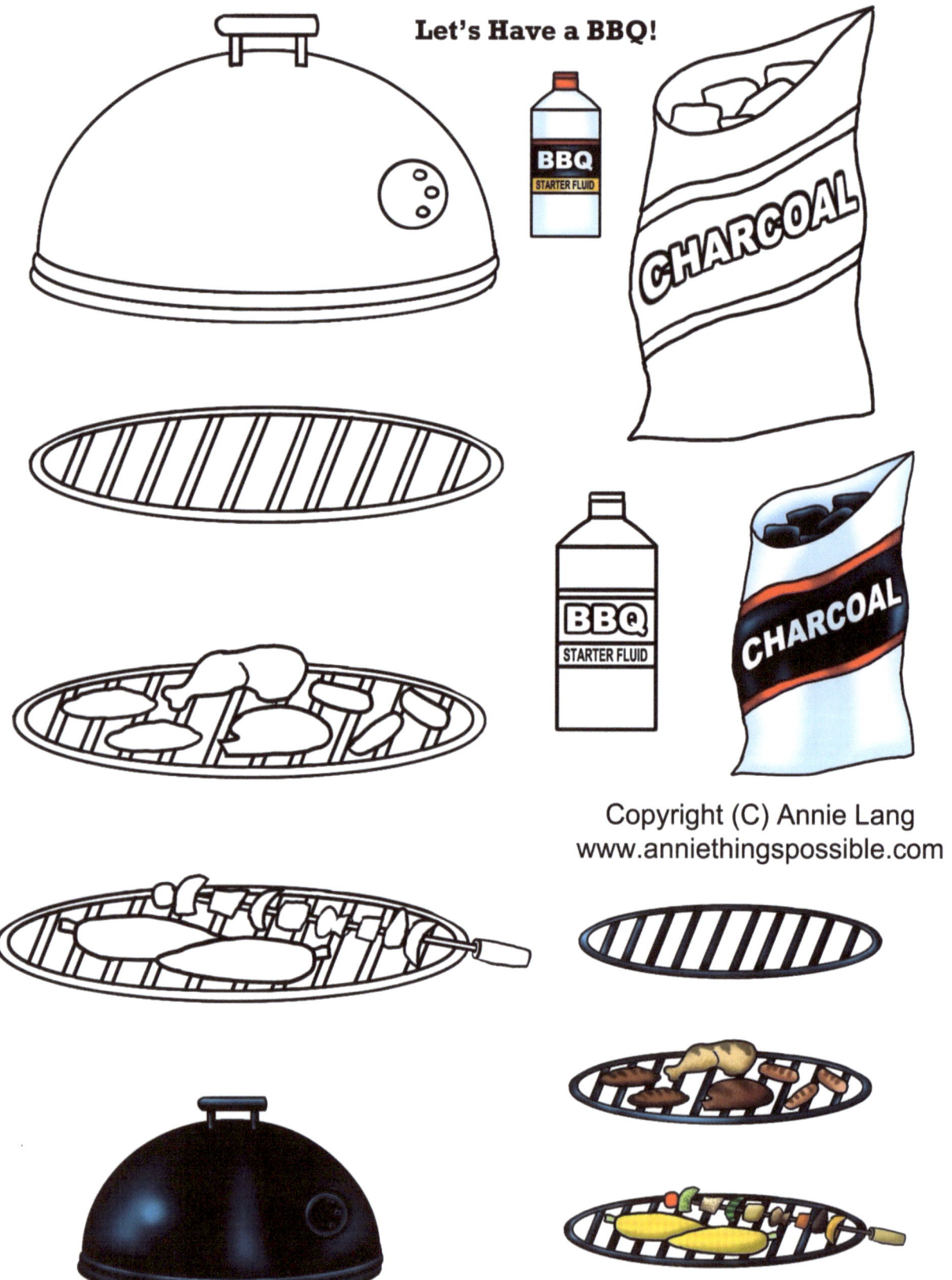

Copyright (C) Annie Lang
www.anniethingspossible.com

Let's Have a BBQ!

Let's Have a BBQ!

Let's Have a BBQ!

Let's Have a BBQ!

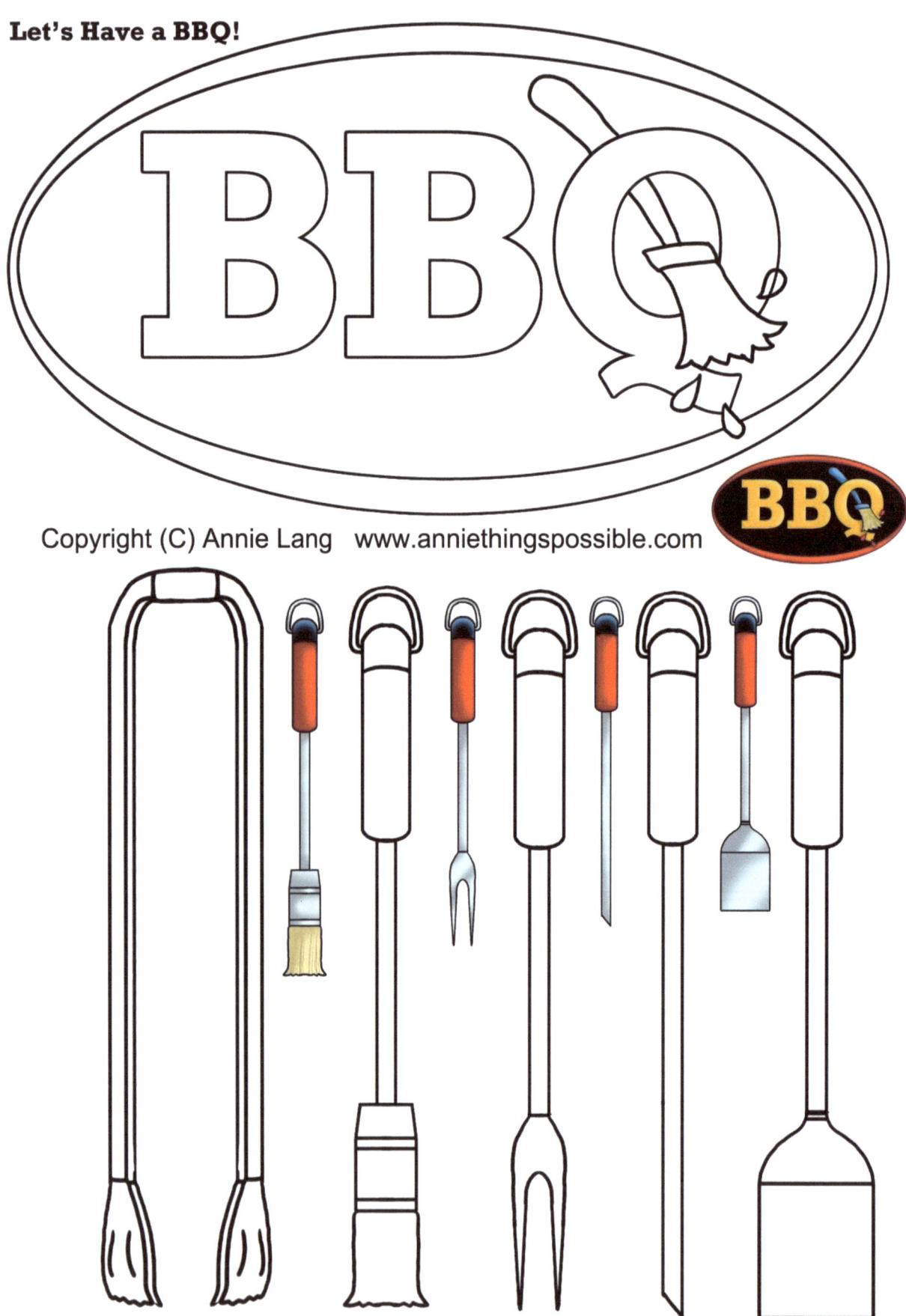

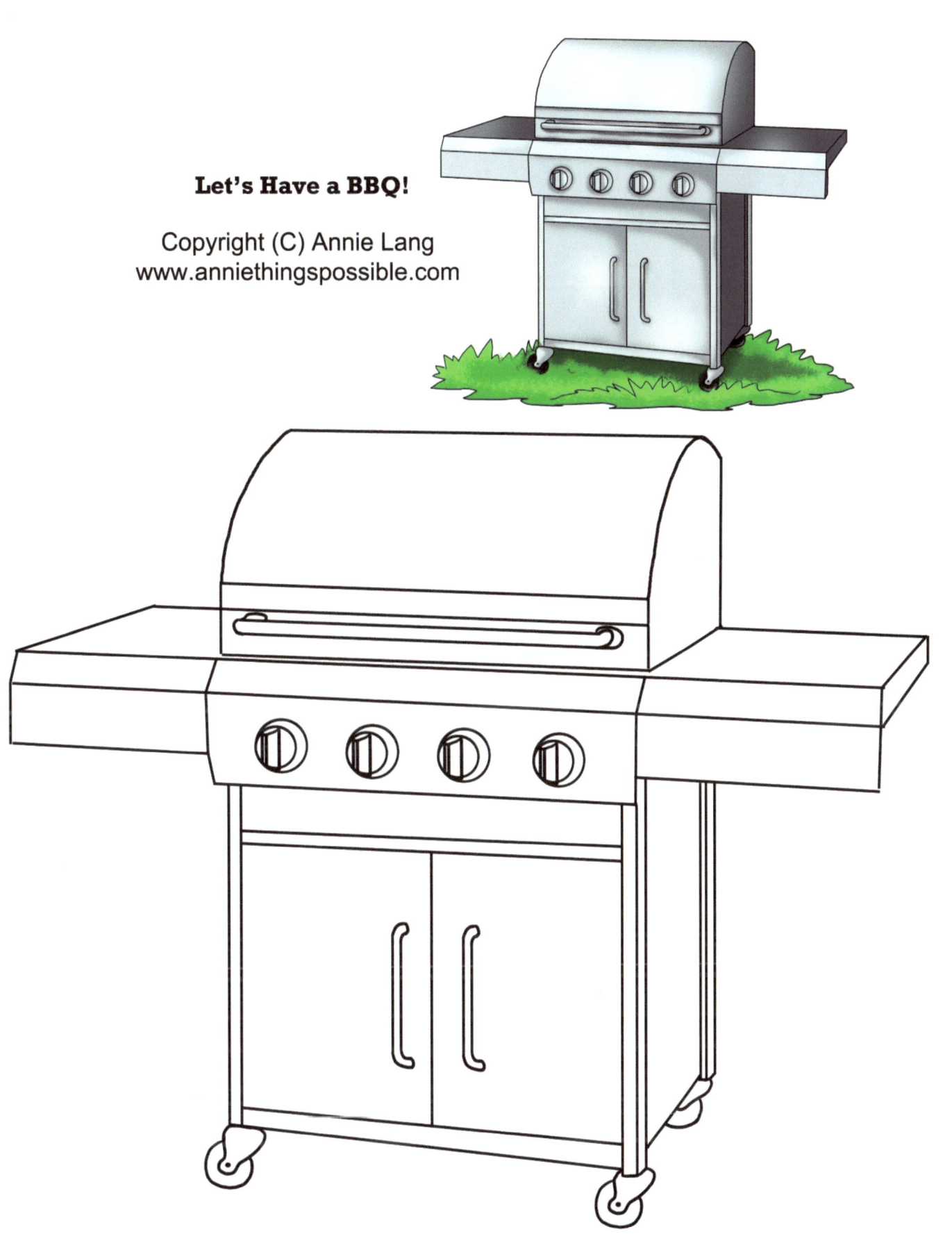

Let's Have a BBQ!

Copyright (C) Annie Lang
www.anniethingspossible.com

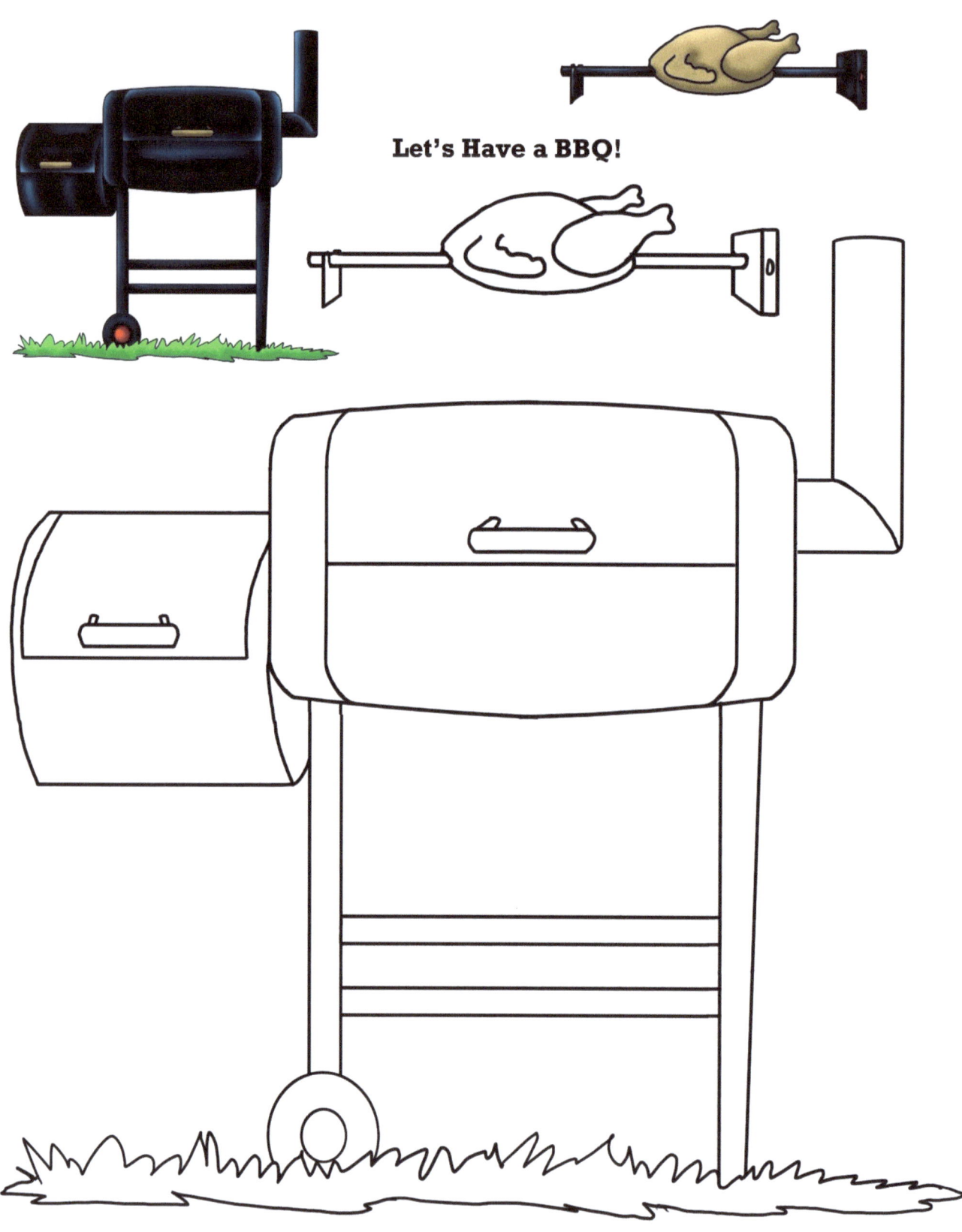

Let's Have a BBQ!

Annie Lang's
BBQ Chickens

"Chick Kabobs"

Annie Lang's
BBQ Chickens

(C) Annie Lang
anniethingspossible.com

"Chicken Salad"

CHARCOAL
BRIQUETTES

CHARCOAL
BRIQUETTES

Annie Lang's
BBQ Chickens

Annie Lang's
BBQ Chickens

"Rotisserie Chickens"

Annie Lang's **BBQ Chickens**

Annie Lang's
BBQ Chickens

(C) Annie Lang
www.anniethingspossible.com

Annie Lang's
BBQ Chickens

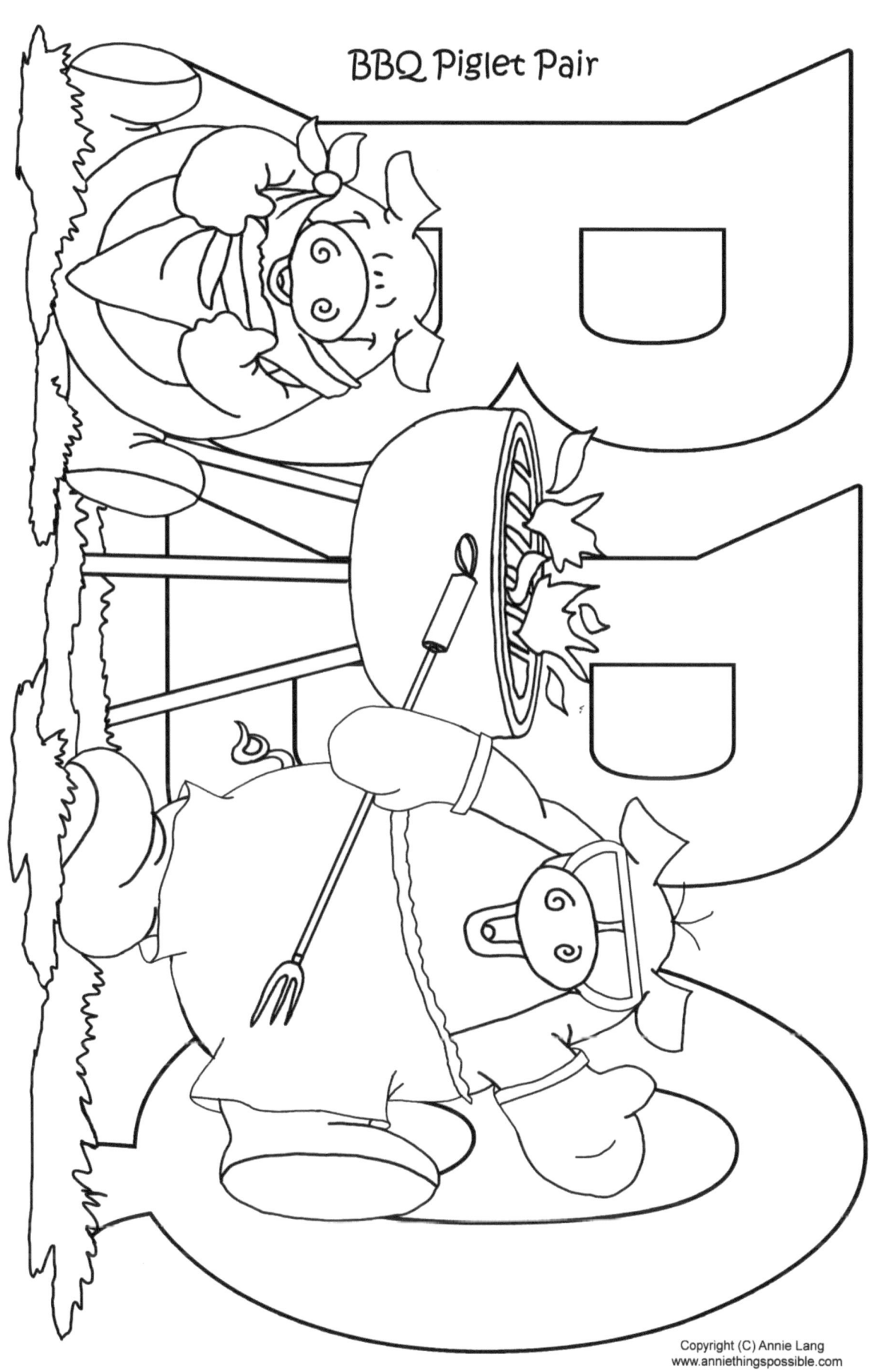

BBQ Piglet Pair

BBQ Piglet
Recipe Card

Marshmallow Piglet

BBQ
Chef
Piglet

Corn Gobbler Piglet

BBQ Helper
Piglet

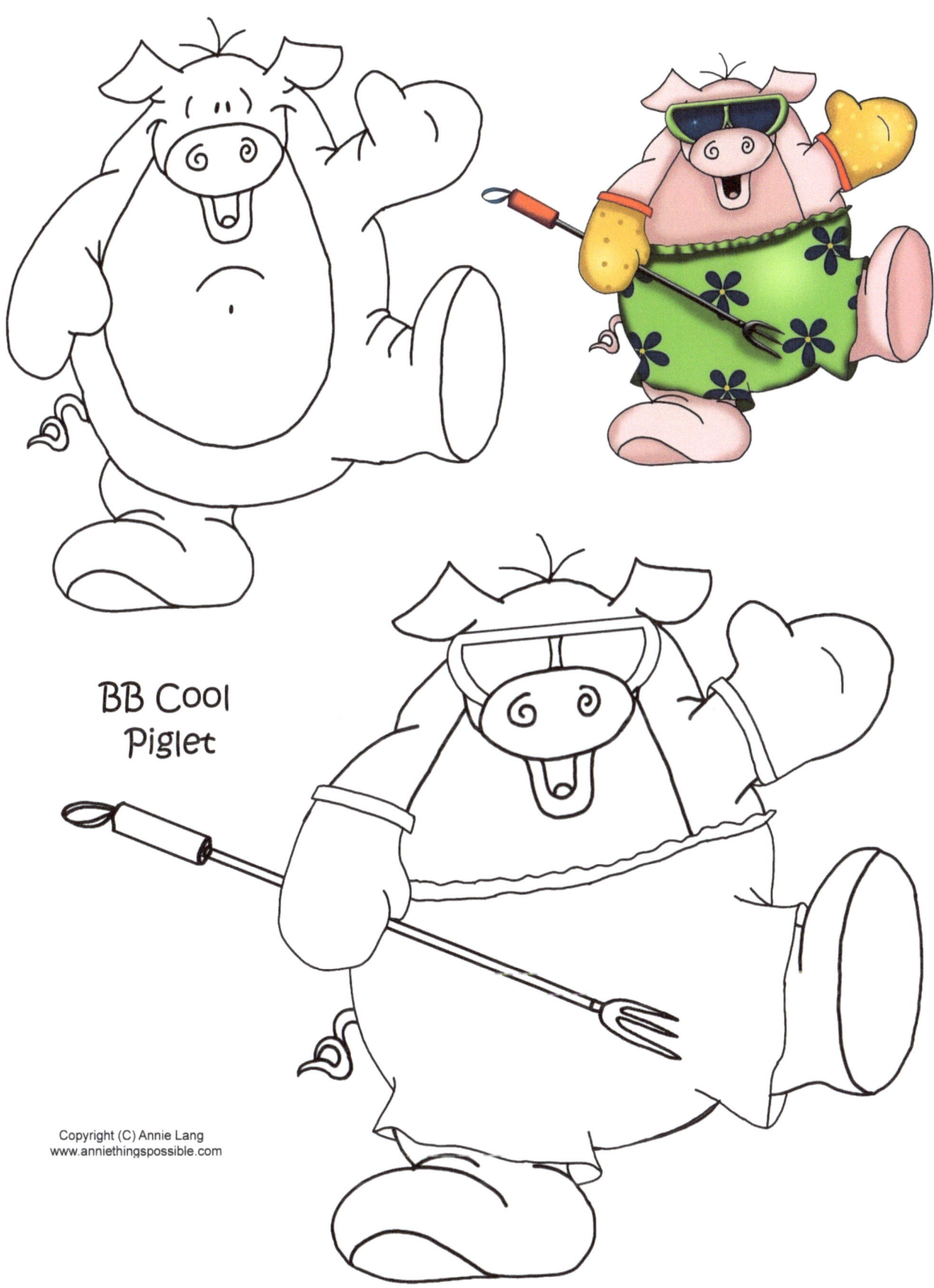

BB Cool
Piglet

Chipster
Piglet

Piglet Sign
Tag or
Label

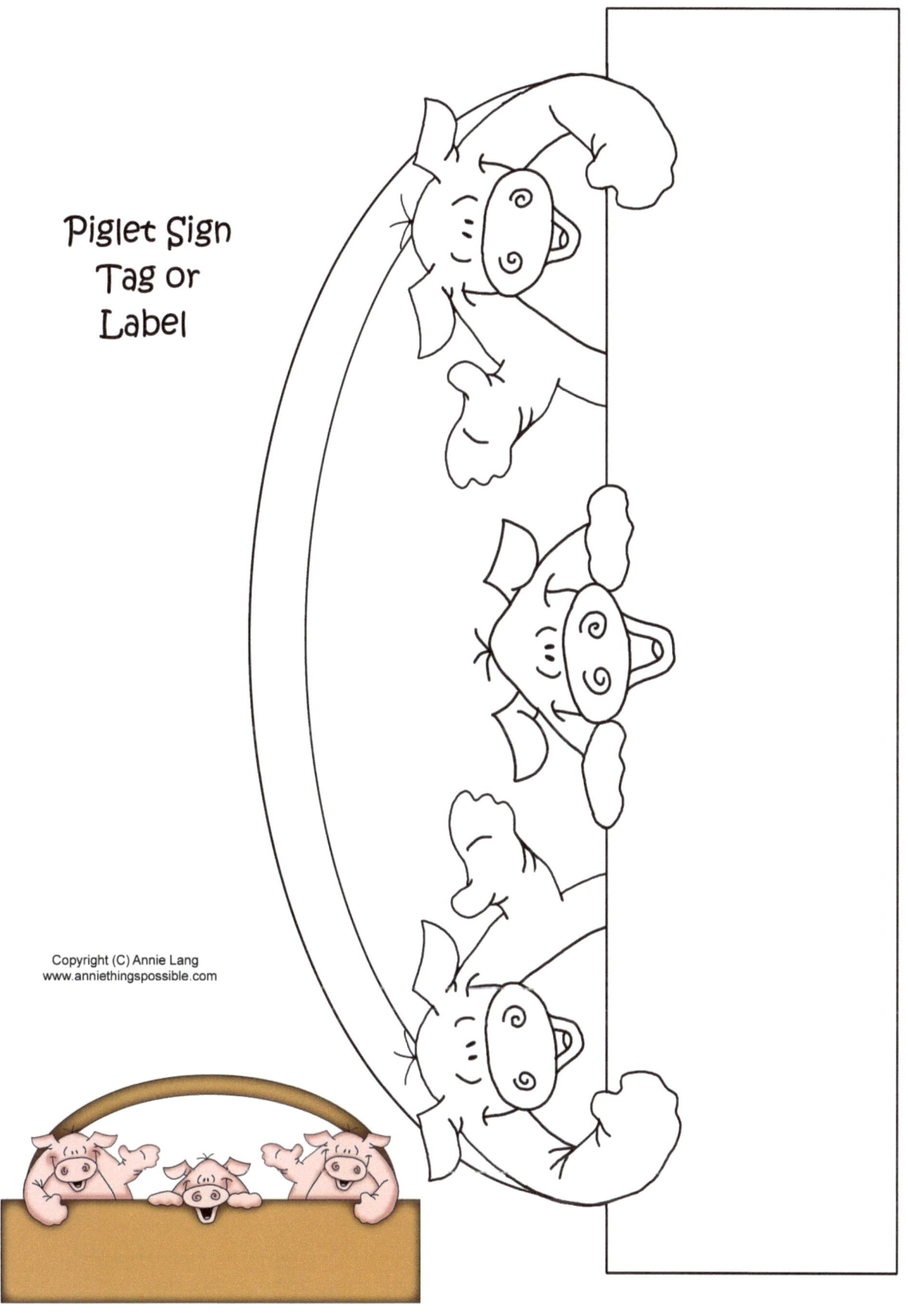

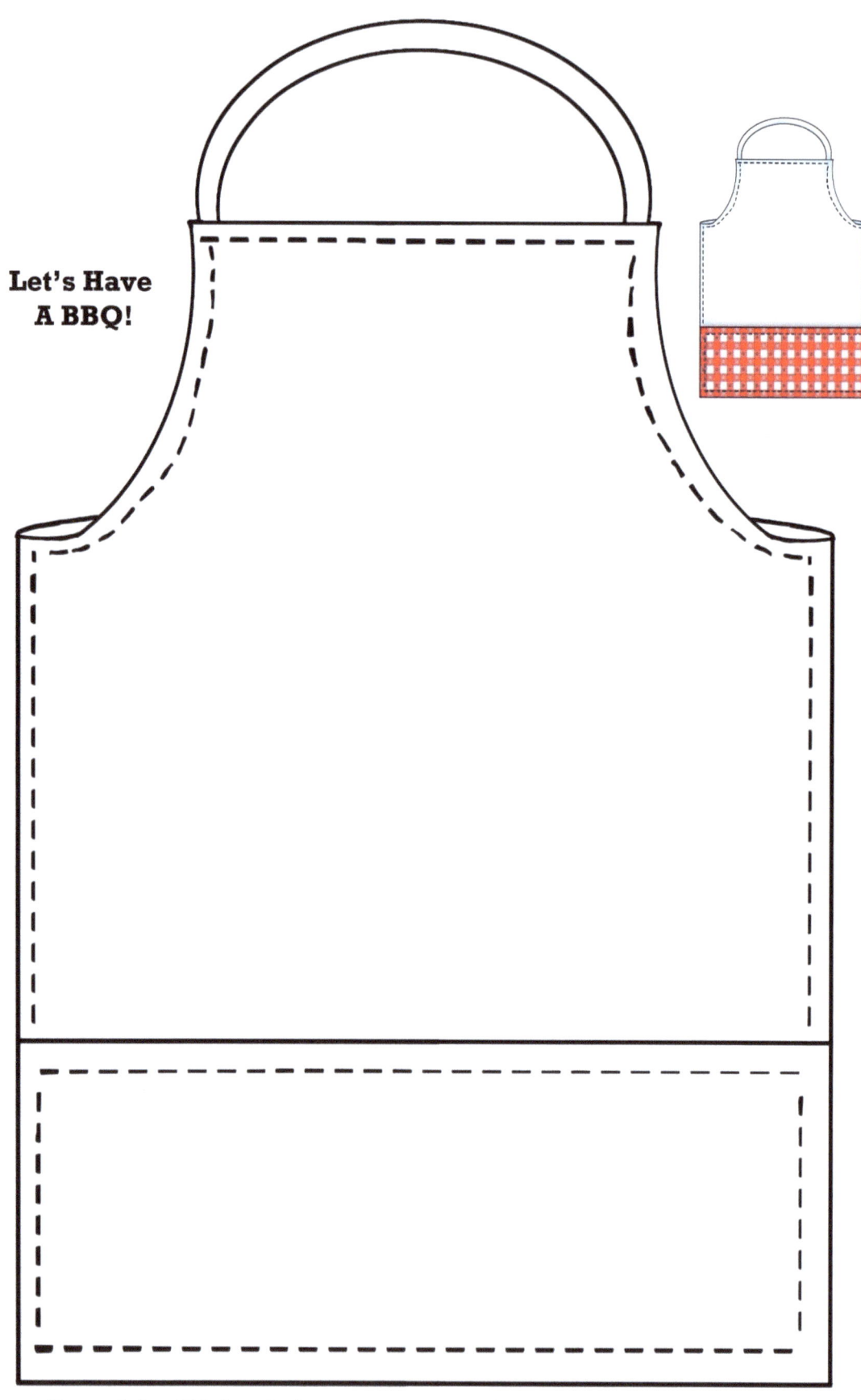

Let's Have A BBQ!

Copyright (C) Annie Lang   www.anniethingspossible.com

notes and memos

Thank you for purchasing this publication!

Find dozens of other fun titles on my
Annie Lang's Books website!

Annie Lang characters, Annie Lang books, Annie Lang art, linework patterns and more!

http://annielangsbooks.com

...it's the place where Annie Things Possible!

*I hope you enjoyed this book and
encourage you to leave a review and share your
thoughts for other customers at Amazon.com!*

*To learn more about the author, get free project
ideas, see video how-to's and more, please visit
Annie Lang's BLOG at
http://annielang-anniethingspossible.blogspot.com/*

anniethingspossible.com
creative designs by Annie Lang

www.ingramcontent.com/pod-product-compliance
Lightning Source LLC
Chambersburg PA
CBHW041527280526
45792CB00004B/1405